Feb. 1991

AUSTRALIA'S GREAT BARRIER REEF

For
Tim, Katee, James, Hugh, Lucinda, Skye, Angus,
Charles & Nicky

Acknowledgements

Photographs: ISOBEL BENNETT, unless otherwise
acknowledged
Artwork: MARTYN ROBINSON B.App.Sc.
Activities: TONI O'NEILL B.Sc., Dip.Ed.
Editor for Series: ANNE BOWER INGRAM O.A.M.
Educational Advisor for Series: Patricia McDonald B.E.M.,
B.Sc., M.Ed., F.M.A.A.
Designer: TREVOR HOOD

COLLINS PUBLISHERS AUSTRALIA
First published in 1987 by William Collins Pty Ltd, Sydney
© Australian Museum, Sydney, 1987
Typeset by Midland Typesetters Pty. Ltd.
First published in paperback 1989
Produced by Mandarin Offset, Hong Kong

National Library of Australia
Cataloguing-in-Publication data:

Bennett, Isobel, 1909–
   The Great Barrier Reef.

ISBN 0 7322 7324 2

   1. Great Barrier Reef (Qld.) Juvenile literature.
   2. Coral reef biology—Queensland—Great Barrier Reef—
      Juvenile literature. I. Australian Museum. II. Title. (Series:
      Australian Museum environment series).

574,9943

THE AUSTRALIAN MUSEUM ENVIRONMENT SERIES

AUSTRALIA'S GREAT BARRIER REEF

Isobel Bennett A.O., M.Sc.

COLLINS
AUSTRALIAN MUSEUM

Great Barrier Reef Region

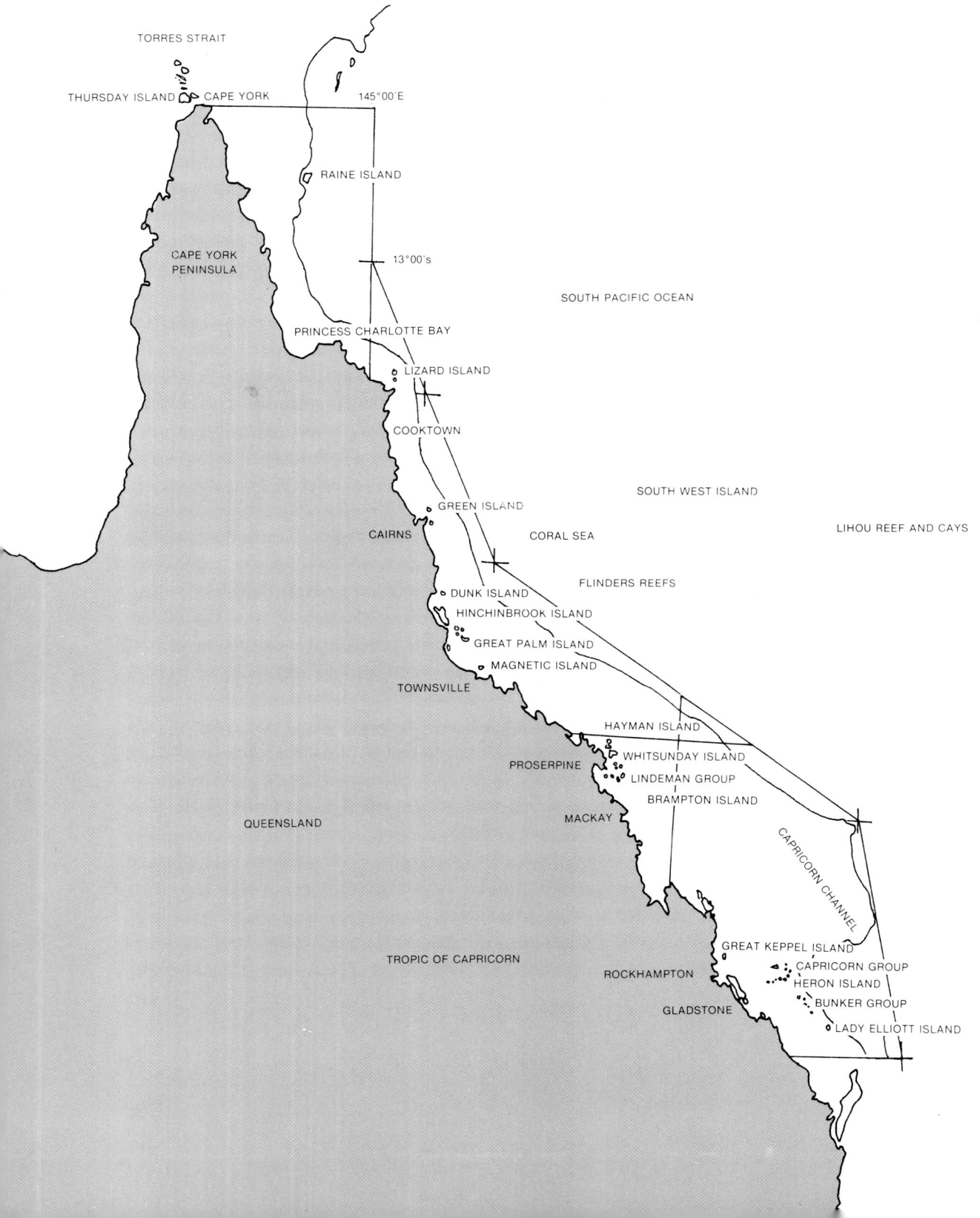

TORRES STRAIT

THURSDAY ISLAND   CAPE YORK

145°00'E

RAINE ISLAND

CAPE YORK PENINSULA

13°00's

SOUTH PACIFIC OCEAN

PRINCESS CHARLOTTE BAY

LIZARD ISLAND

COOKTOWN

GREEN ISLAND

SOUTH WEST ISLAND

CAIRNS

CORAL SEA

LIHOU REEF AND CAYS

FLINDERS REEFS

DUNK ISLAND

HINCHINBROOK ISLAND

GREAT PALM ISLAND

MAGNETIC ISLAND

TOWNSVILLE

HAYMAN ISLAND

WHITSUNDAY ISLAND

PROSERPINE

LINDEMAN GROUP

BRAMPTON ISLAND

QUEENSLAND

MACKAY

CAPRICORN CHANNEL

GREAT KEPPEL ISLAND

TROPIC OF CAPRICORN

CAPRICORN GROUP

ROCKHAMPTON

HERON ISLAND

BUNKER GROUP

GLADSTONE

LADY ELLIOTT ISLAND

Contents

1 The Great Barrier Reef

For most Australians and visitors to this country, the words Great Barrier Reef present a vivid picture, or recall happy memories of a tropical island holiday: clear, sparkling blue-green seas lapping on glistening white sands; wind-surfing and water-skiing; scuba-diving and snorkelling. All this, plus a new and almost unbelievable world of deep blue pools lined with walls of coral exquisite in design, colour and shape, among which bizarre and highly coloured fish flash by in their myriad shoals.

Very few visitors know the fascinating reality of this tremendously complex maze of reefs and islands, for little of the immensity

Sea birds on a coral cay (Photo: John Fields)

and extent of this submarine mountain chain of limestone can be realized or appreciated, even after many visits. It is only from the air, in a low-flying plane, that some of its magic will be glimpsed.

The ever-changing forms, patterns and colours—high, tree-covered continental islands, the low coral cays afloat on the translucent water, the submerged reefs and tiny sandspits, or the ribbons and circles of pale green scattered among the dark blue surrounding sea—these are what go to make up the Great Barrier Reef.

It was Captain Matthew Flinders who first used the word 'barrier' to describe the great series of reefs that stretch in a long line along the far north-eastern Australian coast. That name has been used all over the world now for over two hundred years. However, this name is misleading, it is NOT a single reef, nor is it a series of reefs forming a barrier. Also, it is not a 'barrier reef', that term was first used over one hundred years ago by the famous naturalist, Charles Darwin.

The continental shelf of Queensland, from the Tropic of Capricorn northwards, is unique in the world. Along 2,000 kilometres of its length, and covering an area of over 210,000

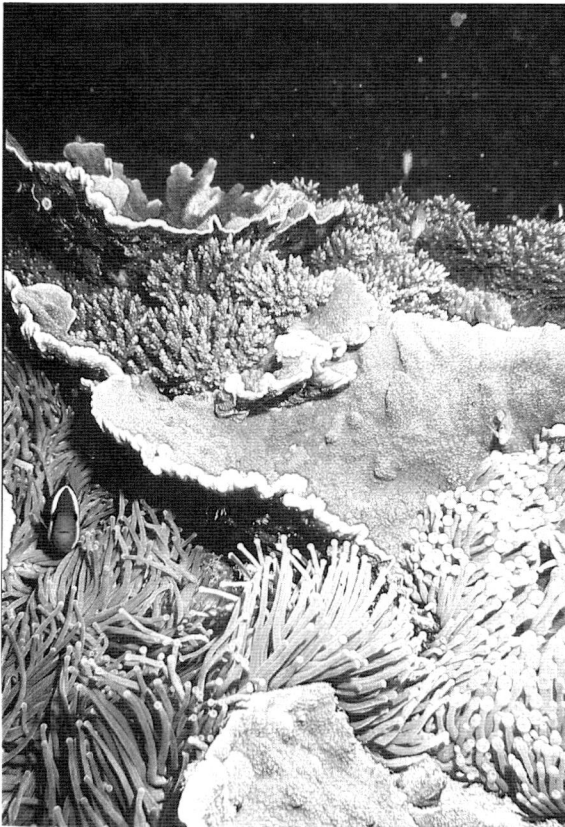

An anemone fish, in its anemone, among coral.
(Photo: L. Zell)

square kilometres, between the latitudes of 9°S. and 24°S., there are scattered innumerable coral reefs and islands. They all lie on and across this narrow shelf, or along its eastern edge, at distances east of the mainland ranging from 24 kilometres to 290 kilometres, in water which varies from a few metres down to 200 metres in depth.

Geologists and geographers studying the continental shelf, and the reefs that have formed on it, are now able to divide these into different kinds, according to their shape and to the nature of their underlying structure.

Subsidence of the continental shelf, and changes of sea level associated with the last ice age have, over the past two million years, altered the depth of water covering the shelf. This variation has affected the rate at which reef-building corals can grow. Today each reef is only a thin cover of living coral overlying a structure made up of dead coral skeletons, the remains of other animals and plants, sand and rubble.

Scientists have drilled bores, to various depths, through several of the reefs in different areas, in order to try and find out the composition of the basic rock on which the original coral polyps settled. The cores that have been obtained have been studied in detail, layer by layer, thus giving a picture of the materials which underlie the reef, and of the rocky base. Knowing the nature of the rock, its geological age can then be assessed.

The climate of the Great Barrier Reef is under the influence both of the land mass of the Australian continent to the west, and the south Pacific Ocean to the east. There is a broad sub-tropical belt of high pressure lying to the east which gives rise to the south-east trade winds. These blow steadily from about February to November. During the late summer months winds may be variable, as this is the season of the north-west monsoon which brings high rainfall to the northern part of the continent. It is also the time of greatest cyclonic activity.

PLAN A TRIP TO THE REEF

There are a hundred different fascinating things to see and do whatever time you visit the reef.

Here are some of the things to take into account when planning a visit:

- South-east trade winds blow fairly constantly from about February to November and temperatures are moderate.
- November to February the weather can be variable. It can be hot and still, raining or even cyclonic.
- However, it is in summer when northerly winds are slight that you may have the clearest water for snorkelling or diving.
- Turtles can be seen nesting and laying eggs from November to February.
- Baby turtles can be seen hatching from January to March.
- Mutton birds (Wedge-tailed Shearwaters), Noddy terns, Gannets and other birds nest from November to January.
- In winter months there are often good day-time extra low tides which makes it an excellent reef-walking time.

When would *you* prefer to visit the reef?   Why?

2 Coral Reefs

In all, there are nearly 3,000 reefs and islands making up the Great Barrier Reef. The islands vary in size, in their height above sea level, and the way in which they were formed. The reefs are solid structures which may be many metres thick below the floor of the sea surrounding them. These coral reefs are probably the most extensive series that has ever existed, and almost certainly the largest structures on earth today created by living organisms.

These reefs have been built up by millions of minute plants and animals, layer by layer, through geological time. Today's living reefs are a thin veneer on a limy substrate of coral skeletons and other reef animals and plants.

Coral reefs are formed originally by the lowliest of animals—tiny, fragile, jelly-like polyps, which are able to secrete hard, limy skeletons of calcium carbonate. With few exceptions these reefs are only found within the tropics, for the reef-building corals are restricted to warm, shallow tropical waters.

Normally, flourishing coral growth does not take place below a depth of about sixty metres, although recently reef-building corals have been discovered at depths around 200 metres on northern outer Barrier reefs. The best conditions range from about five to thirty metres, with a water temperature between 20°C. and 30°C.

Within this depth and temperature range, in clear oceanic water, reef-building corals may settle and flourish, wherever conditions for their growth are favourable. The temperature must remain fairly constant and there needs to be a plentiful supply of food substances which are constantly renewed by waters rich in oxygen and calcium.

Reef-building corals, unlike those found in deep, colder waters, have microscopic single-celled plants within their tissues. These are known as *Zooxanthellae*. There are also tiny green filamentous algae (seaweeds) within the calcareous, limy skeletons of the corals. In recent years these minute plants have been discovered to aid both as food producers, and in skeleton building.

These microscopic plants need sunlight to enable them to convert the inorganic salts of the sea into food material. So, the depth to which sunlight can penetrate the sea water, is the main factor restricting the depth at which reef-building corals can grow.

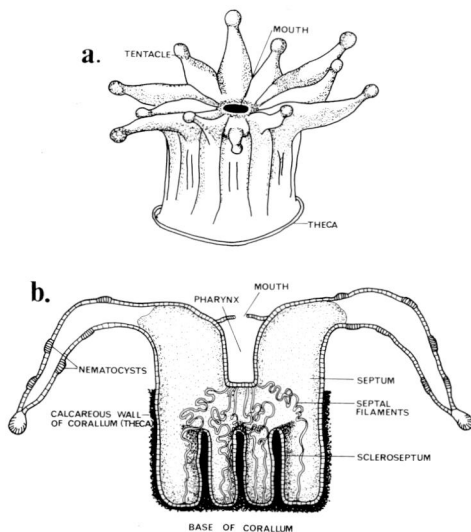

Diagram to illustrate the structure of a single coral polyp.
a) as seen from the outside
b) a section cut through the polyp—the black parts are part of the calcareous skeleton.
Polyps may vary in size from less than a millimetre to several centimetres, according to the species, and also vary in the number of tentacles, usually multiples of six. In some of the massive corals, the polyps have become very elongated and then may have more than one mouth.

This is a very interesting example showing the development of a Mushroom coral, as there are as many as 50 little skeletons in different stages of growth. The Mushroom corals do not form colonies, they are all single individuals. When the planula larva first settles, it secretes a stalk (clearly seen at the top of the picture), by which it is attached to the substrate (here the bottom of a large dead mushroom coral). It gradually reaches a stage where it becomes so large that it breaks off the stalk and continues to grow lying on the reef among other corals or in sandy pools.

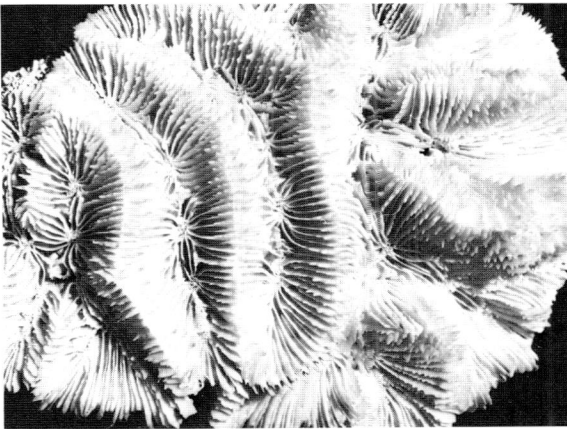

Skeleton of part of a colony of a Brain coral. In this coral each polyp has several mouths, and the position of these can be seen lying along the grooves.

SUNLIGHT THROUGH WATER

Finding out about the light corals receive:

- Find something red (red plastic is best).
- Look at its colour in the sunlight.
- Hold it under water and check its colour.
- Dive down and look at its colour under water.

(The red wavelengths in sunlight don't penetrate water as far as other wavelengths, so the deeper you dive, the less red your object will look.)

3 Coral Cays

The word 'Cay' is the name given to the true coral islands and is the equivalent of the word 'Key' used in the Caribbean Sea. Some are just sandbanks with no grass cover. Others vary from a sparse cover of grasses, creepers and low shrubs to tall trees.

These coral cays are of great importance as the resting places and breeding grounds of many species of seabirds, (a few are amongst the most important in the world). In the summer months, they are also a breeding ground for certain kinds of marine turtles.

When reef-building corals have grown upwards to a sea level height, where they are exposed to air at low tide, the corals on the upper surface of the reef begin to die off.

West Riversong Cay, Swain Reefs.
A bare sandbank with numbers of resting birds, and no vegetation of any kind.

One Tree Island, Capricorn Group.
One of only eight cays composed entirely of coral shingle instead of sand and sediment.

Coral colonies continue only to grow outwards, horizontally, round the edges of the reef. With the passing of time, the dead coral is broken off by the pounding of waves and eventually is reduced to small fragments of rubble.

Further pounding and breaking up reduces this rubble, together with the remains of plants, mollusc shells and other reef animals, into finer particles. These sediments are carried by currents, wind and wave action, across the reef to a more protected area on the leeward side. Here they gradually accumulate into banks of sand.

Once these sandbanks become stabilized, and have been built up to a level where they remain uncovered during periods of high water, various seabirds begin to take advantage of them as resting places and later as nesting sites. From the bird droppings a layer of organic humus is gradually formed, making land space available for colonization by plants. These will be species which have either salt-resistant seeds, that may be blown, or drift there, by winds and currents, or have been carried there by birds. Only those plants which are highly specialized for living in limy soils and being constantly covered in salt spray, are able to survive.

Seed pods of different kinds, strewn along the sandy shores of coral cays, show a means by which many plant species are dispersed over large areas of sea.

WHAT IS A CAY MADE OF?

If you are visiting a coral cay, walk around it and find the area where the coarsest sand or coral rubble can be found. Pick up a small container full and sort through it. Try to identify each piece. Fill in this list:

- plant
- mollusc shells
- staghorn coral
- honeycomb coral
- red organ pipe coral

- other corals
- forams
- bits of other animals
- can't identify

4 The 'High' Islands

The islands of the Great Barrier Reef are not all low coral cays.

There are high, hilly almost mountainous islands, with rocky tree-clad cliffs, or gentle slopes rolling down to the seashore. The greatest number of these extend in groups for several hundred kilometres, mainly to the east of the Queensland cities of Bowen and Mackay.

These islands vary in distance from the mainland coast, from a few kilometres to over 100 kilometres. They are generally referred to as 'high', 'continental' or 'mainland' islands because they are composed of rocks and other materials of the same composition and geological ages as the continent itself, with similar trees and other plants.

These 'high' islands are the exposed remnants of now submerged coastal ranges, which were cut off in the past by a change in sea level and remain as the islands of today.

There are over 600 islands of this kind and there is a great variety of natural habitats to be found on them. These range from rocky outcrops on the shore to sandy beaches or mangrove swamps and, where conditions in the sea have favoured the settlement of coral larvae, there are near-shore or 'fringing' reefs.

A fringing reef on Border Island, Whitsunday Group.
A "High" Island where every dead boulder is a shelter for a host of animals.

5 The Coral Reef Community

On a visit to the Great Barrier Reef, it is important to know and appreciate at least a little about the reefs and their flora and fauna. Each part of a reef has its own special association of plants and animals whether it be a deep coral pool, a shallow sandy flat, a mangrove glade, the seaward slope of the reef, or the beach rock along the sandy shore of a cay.

Colourful living corals will only be seen out on the far seaward edges, or in deep coral pools along the edge, or round the margins of a lagoon within a reef, NOT on a sandy or seaweed-covered rubble flat near a cay or a larger island.

Also, it should be remembered that there are hundreds of dead boulder tracts and sandy flats on the reefs and that it is possible to walk along some reefs without seeing any coral at all, unless the right zones are visited.

The coral reef community is the most complex and diverse in the sea; it can be compared to an extensive and luxuriant tropical rain forest. Within the narrow limits of a reef, there is a greater variety of animals and plants than anywhere else in the sea. There are literally billions of organisms—from the ultramicroscopic to large fishes, reptiles, birds and mammals. They are all dependent in some way on one another, and they all exist together in harmonious balance within this one ecological system.

Every single member of a coral reef community has some part to play in the very complex food webs that link them. The plants absorb energy from the sun and transform the inorganic materials in the sea into food for all the herbivorous (plant-eating) species. Each of these in turn, from the smallest to the largest, provides food for the carnivores (the flesh-eaters). Eggs and larval stages of many marine animals—sponges, corals, anemones, worms, crabs and lobsters, sea shells, starfish, sea urchins, fish and others—not only provide food for other animals, but during the time they spend drifting about in the sea as members of the floating 'plankton' community, they are also being carried from reef to reef. Thus populations on one reef may be replenished from another reef. Different species are distributed along the whole region, either from one reef to the next, or from the nearby Pacific and Indian Oceans.

It is not possible, even today, to name a single Barrier Reef animal about which *everything* is known—all the details of its life history, its full relationship to other reef animals or plants, and its geographical range. Much more attention has been paid to some groups of animals than to others.

Diagram of coral inhabitants

6 The Coral Cay Community

The plant life of most of the high, continental islands closely resembles that of the nearby mainland. However, on the coral cays, especially in the southern parts of the Reef, the plant life consists of species that are only found in that particular habitat.

The three important factors which limit the kinds of plants able to survive on coral islands are: the limy (calcareous) nature of the soils; the extremely unstable nature of the beaches (geologists have shown that cyclonic activity may cause the removal of hundreds of tonnes of sand from the beaches thus reducing the size of the cay); the high salt content, both in the soil and in the air.

A very good example of the gradual development of a coral island community is to be seen in the cays of the Capricorn Group, which range from bare sandbanks, visible only at low tide, to densely tree-covered cays, such as Heron Island.

Along the top of the shoreline the first arrivals are the coarse grasses, the wild Convolvulus, and other creepers. On isolated cays far out on the Barrier Reef, even plants such as these have a hard fight for survival, since the whole land surface may carry enormous numbers of nesting seabirds.

With time, the humus of decaying plants and the bird droppings form a soil able to support shrubs and finally larger trees. The first of the trees seen on a walk across an island is the graceful Casuarina, which usually

Heron Island, Capricorn Group.
Pisonia trees, the largest and most beautiful trees to be found on coral cays.

Casuarina or she-oak

forms an outer fringe round the cay. Under its slight protection from wind-blown spray, two other smaller trees flourish. The shapely spreading Tournefortia is easily recognized by its silvery-grey leaves and creamy flowers, which are important as they attract nectar-feeding insects to these isolated cays. The second is the smaller *Scaevola*, sometimes called the Cardwell Cabbage, which has shiny green leaves and tiny white flowers.

Once these trees are well established, the environment becomes more stable and enables the development of others. The Screw or Pandanus Palm, with its fascinating prop roots and large fruits, which are bright orange when ripe, is one of the best-known

Cardwell Cabbage

One of the most characteristic trees of a coral cay, the *Pandanus* palm has prop roots which are necessary to support the top-heavy crown of leaves and heavy fruit so often seen on these trees.

and most characteristic trees of the coral island shores. Since its seeds seem to need shaded conditions to develop, it is not usually found along the outer edge, except in areas where considerable erosion and cyclonic activity have taken place removing the outer tree cover.

The Sandpaper Fig Tree and the Native Mulberry, whose seeds are carried by birds, easily become established. Finally, with further ground cover, humus and the accumulated droppings of thousands of nesting seabirds, the soil of the coral cay becomes favourable for the growth of the large *Pisonia* tree. This magnificent tree is only found in this environment. In places it becomes a forest, a dense canopy of green with the sunlight filtering through its large bright leaves.

The scene may be different on far northern cays, which lie closer to the mainland, and on which there may be quite extensive mangrove glades. On the eastern margin of the Low Isles reef, which lies about fourteen kilometres north-east of the town of Port Douglas, there is a large mangrove cay. Three different kinds

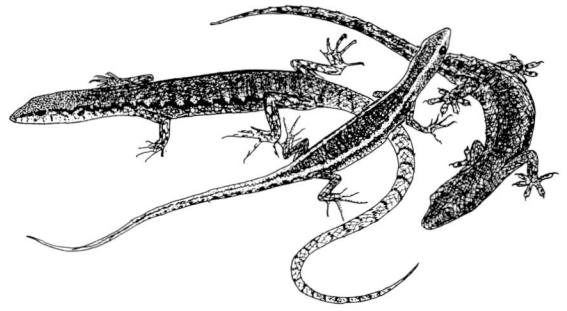

Lizards of Coral Cays

of mangrove are found there, growing in soil that ranges from pure sand to deep mangrove mud. The animals living among it vary in the same way, with Corals and Cowry shells among the mangrove roots in the sand, and mud creepers and small mud-dwelling crabs at the other extreme.

Since mangrove swamps are characteristic of the mainland shores in these latitudes, the proximity of the reefs to the coast makes them readily accessible to colonization by mangrove seedlings carried there by the tides and currents.

Because most of the coral cays are a considerable distance from the mainland of

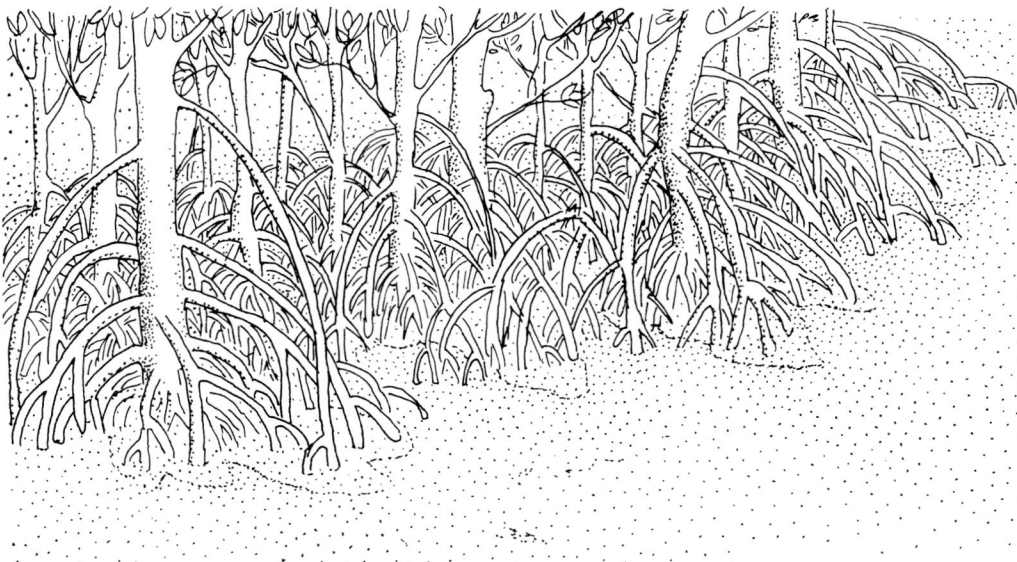

Mangroves (*Rhizophora*) with their prop roots

16

Queensland, it is not surprising that none of the common larger animals, apart from the birds, is found. A small house gecko and two little skink lizards have been recorded, but they have almost certainly been brought there, probably accidentally, by man.

There are, however, quite large numbers of insects and spiders, most of which have by some means or other, reached the cays from the mainland. They may have arrived on floating objects washed ashore, or carried on aerial currents and wind, on birds and by man, especially where there is a tourist resort or camping ground on a cay.

Among the insects the butterflies are the most noticeable. They are easily carried by aerial currents and wind, but their actual survival on the islands depends on the availability of suitable food.

As many as sixty different kinds of spiders have been found on the cays of the Capricorn and Bunker Groups. These animals are carnivorous, able to eat a wide variety of small invertebrates and they are able to survive quite a long time without food and so have become successful colonizers on the islands.

Insects and spiders of coral cays

MAKE A PLANT MAP

If you are staying on a coral cay draw an outline of your island. Try to work out N, S, E and W on your map.

Now start to walk around the island and record the plants at the edge of the sand.

Find out:

- Do different plants grow on different sides of the island?
- Can you think why?
- Find a track and walk through the island.
- Draw on your map the plants you find along the track.

7 The Sandy Beach

Surrounding the coral cay there is usually a sandy beach which may be a mixture of fine white coral sand and areas of larger particles of coral, broken and dead shells and remains of other animals. During the day, the only obvious features are large holes, which are the burrows of the Ghost Crab. This beach scavenger comes out at night to feed.

Among the most common of the dead shells are the small, very hard, white triangular single valves of the Eugerie (or Pippi), or the ribbed shells of the Heart Cockle. Both these molluscs live burrowed down in the sand just beyond the beach itself, and they are preyed upon by birds and fishes.

If you were to dig in the sand near the water's edge you could find large numbers of small Bristle worms which live there. Also, there is a tiny red, white-spotted Sea Cucumber, which lies buried just below the surface.

Dramatic tracks seen at dawn on a coral cay. Not the marks of a huge tractor, but the tracks made by a large female turtle as she returns to the sea after laying her eggs high up on the shore above the beach.

In the summer months, from October to about February, the beach may look as though a tractor has been across it. The tracks are those of a large female turtle who has come ashore to lay her eggs high up above the sand.

High up on the sand beaches of coral cays the most important dwellers are the Ghost Crabs. By day, the only signs of their presence are the large holes scattered along the beach. These crabs prey on the little turtle hatchlings as they emerge from their nests at night during the late summer months. With the aid of a torch, the crabs are easily seen at night. They have strangely shaped, long stalked eyes, and they move with lightning speed.

8 The Beach Rock

Heron Island, showing a large area of beach rock in the foreground.

On a number of Barrier Reef coral cays there may be a long stretch of rocky shore along the edge of the sandy beach, which is generally known as beach rock.

The amount of beach rock to be seen on any cay may vary considerably from year to year, according to weather conditions. Cyclones may either cover or uncover quite large areas as wave action moves the sand.

This beach rock is composed of calcareous sand and reef debris, which have been cemented into a solid structure under certain physical conditions, but its actual composition varies. Along its upper edge the beach rock may be fairly soft, and as it crumbles its nature can be easily seen. Nearer the water it may often be very hard and jagged, and difficult to walk on.

Here you will find animals which normally don't occur on other parts of the reef. Only where there are large boulders tossed up by cyclones along a reef edge, which are at the same tidal level as the beach rock, do you find such animals as oysters, barnacles and coat-of-mail shells.

Small periwinkles occur in large numbers along the upper edge of the beach rock. When the tide comes in they spread out to feed on the minute algae (seaweeds) growing on the rocky surface. At the ends, where the rock merges into the land, there may be groups of small Clusterwinks huddled together to conserve moisture at low tide.

9 The Reef Flat

Heron Island, northern shore, showing the reef flat, a safe and rewarding hunting ground for the reef-walker.

Seaward of the sloping sandy beach or the beach rock (where this is present), there is usually a broad expanse of sandy flat which is a safe and very fascinating place to begin exploring the reef.

It may be a very extensive area which can often be divided into an inner and outer zone. Usually it is a mixture of sandy areas, dead coral rubble and coral boulders, some of which are living and some dead. Dead boulders usually have a covering of various kinds of brown or green seaweeds.

Since the surface of the reef flat varies a little in level, the water covering it may vary in depth from a few centimetres to over a metre, even during the lowest spring tides. The water gradually gets deeper as you wander out towards the edge of the reef.

The living colonies of coral on the inshore reef flat are those which are able to withstand a wide range of conditions, such as very high temperatures in summer coinciding with low tides, or low salinity after continuous heavy rain.

Scattered everywhere over sandy parts of the reef flat there may be numbers of large black sea cucumbers, or sometimes the more colourful pink and brown ones. These animals feed on the floor of the flats—they ingest the sand, remove the organic food particles, and pass out the remains as little coils of sand.

Sand-plough snails and purple-mouthed stromb shells are found on these sandy areas. The snails are carnivores, eating mainly small

Sea Cucumbers feeding on the sandy shallow of a reef flat. As the Sea Cucumber ingests the sand, it removes the organic food particles and leaves behind it little coils of sand.

bivalve molluscs. They bore holes through the shell by means of their strong teeth, aided by an acid secretion. These animals are easily seen as you explore the reef flat but, out of sight, buried in the sand, thousands of other reef dwellers live out their lives.

Although the common garden earthworm is never associated with the sea, research workers at Heron Island recorded five different species of marine worms related to this group. These tiny worms live in the sand under and around coral boulders on the reef flat, and they have been found in numbers up to 20,000 in one square metre.

A research worker there in the 1970s found over 1400 tiny Bristle worms, belonging to 103 different species, in one small clump of coral that weighed only four and a half kilograms.

Worms of every kind are found— swimming, crawling on the reef flat, burrowing, sheltering under boulders, or among coral rubble, or living in tubes of their own making.

There are Flatworms, Ribbon worms, and ringed or segmented Bristle worms. Many are strikingly marked, or brilliantly iridescent as

Flatworm. This colourful species is often seen gliding over coral or swimming in sandy pools on the reef flat.

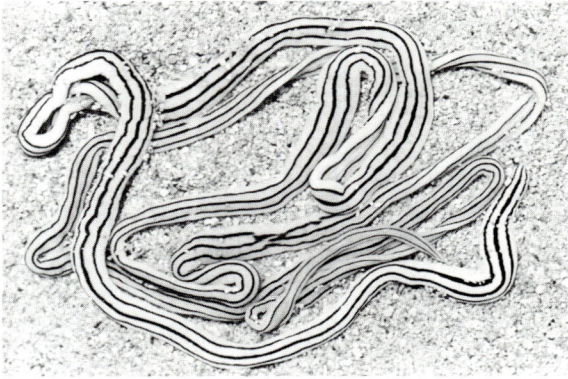

A Ribbon worm found among the coral rubble on the reef flat. This worm, when fully extended, was nearly one and a half metres in length.

the light catches on the chitinous outer layer of the body.

Among the covering of brown and green seaweeds on the boulders there may be large rounded clumps of a brown sponge. However, it is on the undersides of these boulders, and in the sandy substrate below them, that the most exciting animals may be found.

The soft, felted tubes of a large tubeworm can often be seen attached to the underside of the boulders. Its long white, thread-like tentacles spread out over the sand or boulder, are often the only indication of its presence. A large grey Bristle worm, with rows of tiny rusty-red gills at the base of each bunch of bristles, lives in the sand, also, the File shell, which has long bright red mantle processes. By flapping the two valves of its shell this little mollusc is able to swim, and rapidly tries to return to the shelter of the boulder when disturbed.

As you wade through slightly deeper water over the outer flat towards the reef edge, more and more colonies of living coral may be found with a greater variety of species.

Suddenly there is a brilliant splash of colour which disappears as you approach. Then you see the two white tips of the shell of a large

Tubeworms have a mass of long, thread-like white tentacles, which spread out over the substrate collecting organic food particles from the sand.

Clam wedged down among the corals. The fleshy part of the animal, which is visible between the shell valves, is known as the mantle. There is an amazing array of colour to be seen in the mantles, ranging from vivid greens, blues and purples, to fawn, brown and black, in all combinations.

The clams are unique among the molluscs of the reefs. Like the corals, the clams have microscopic algae (*Zooxanthellae*) within their tissues, which manufacture a large part of the food of these filter-feeding animals. Since these minute algae need sunlight like all other plants, there are special lens-like structures on the surface of the mantle which allow the sunlight to penetrate deep into the animal tissue. This is the reason these large molluscs are always to be seen, either attached to the substrate or lying on the sand, with the shell valves open and the mantles expanded to receive the maximum sunlight.

The small burrowing clam and its slightly

Green seaweed (*Halimeda*) is one of the easily identified algae attached to boulders on the reef flat.

larger relative, *Tridacna maxima*, are found on most reefs, but the much larger Horse's Foot and Giant clams are only found on the more northern reefs, and usually in deeper water.

Dark green Mantis Shrimps dart for cover at great speed as you walk across the corals. Crabs of every shape and colour scuttle for

Reef clam. The mantle colours can range from fawns, browns and black, to brilliant greens, blues and purples.

shelter. The large, very sluggish Curry Fish, which is a fawn-coloured Sea Cucumber, and the beautiful Tiger Cowry, live on this part of the reef flat. Fawn-coloured starfish browse on the coral rubble together with the Red-lipped Stromb shells, which are often mistaken for Cone shells. The Strombs are easily distinguished from Cones by the groove in the lip of the shell.

Large Pin-cushion Starfish, which don't look like starfish until you turn them over, may be found on the sandy floor of pools. This starfish, like its relative, the Crown-of-Thorns, is a carnivore and feeds on coral. Fortunately it is a solitary animal, not seen occurring in great numbers like its formidable relative.

As one wades across the reef flat, small sand-coloured fishes, gobies and blennies, dart for cover. A tiny Box Fish cruises slowly around a coral pool, or small black and white Humbugs dart in and out among the coral. A

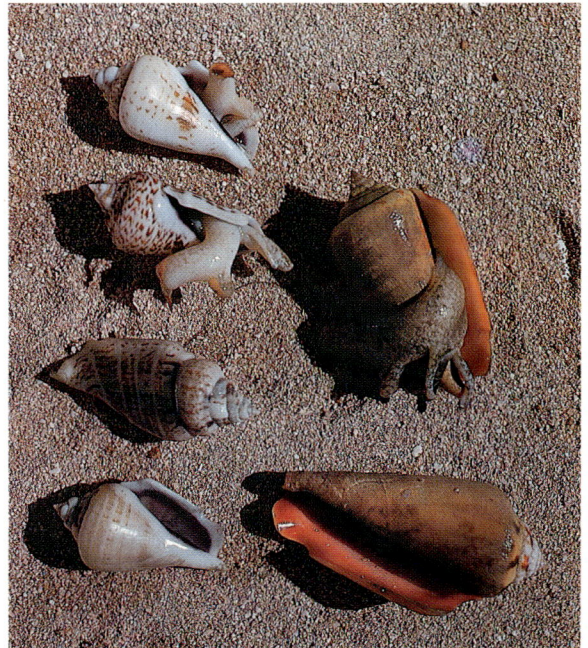

Stromb shells are common on the surface of the inner reef flats—the Purple-mouth on the sandy areas and the Red-lip on the rubble areas to seaward.

The Crown-of-Thorns starfish feeds on living coral and has become a serious menace on the Great Barrier Reef.

Shoals of browsing Parrot fishes invade the reef flat as the tide comes in. (Photo: Ron & Valerie Taylor)

beautifully marked little Epaulette shark, up to about a metre long, lurks among the corals. It is historically interesting as being the first shark recorded from Australian waters. It was described by members of Captain Cook's crew from the Endeavour River.

A Blue-spotted ray may shoot from underfoot with the speed of lightning. With the returning tide, shoals of brilliantly coloured Parrot fishes invade the reef, to begin feeding on the minute algae on the boulders.

Marks made by the Parrot fish 'beaks' when feeding on coral.

A REEF FLAT WALK

You can be sure to see something different on every reef walk you take. Keep a diary of the most interesting things you see. Be careful where you walk so you don't break the coral. If you handle anything be gentle and make sure it goes back in the same place it came from.

Your Reef Flat Diary could include:

- The date of your walk.
- Notes on animals and plants you found.
- Interesting records like how many different kinds of seastars or corals you found.

10 The Boulder Zone

Boulder Zone, Green Island Reef, with a giant clam in foreground and a blue coral pool beyond.

On some reefs, such as that along the northern edge of Heron Island, the area of living corals in deeper water of the reef flat merges into a higher region consisting of large dead coral boulders. This can be a very rich and rewarding hunting ground for reef fossickers.

Under these often rainbow-coloured boulders an enormous number of small or microscopic animals live out their lives, protected both from the heat of the sun and from predators. Encrusting sponges, small tubeworms, Bryozoans and Colonial Ascidians (tiny sea squirts), may cover the whole of the undersurface of a boulder.

Boulders. The undersides of boulders provide excellent homes for thousands of minute reef animals.

Brittle Star. This beautifully marked green brittle star is the largest found in Barrier Reef waters.

Boulders. Here a Cowry is seen laying its eggs in capsules which then attach to the underside of the boulder.

Hermit crabs, living in little dead mollusc shells, scuttle in the sand. Small shrimps, a large mollusc, a Cowry laying its eggs in the spring, a large beautiful green Brittle Star, little crabs, large Sea Hares. What you find is all a matter of luck, depending on the boulder you choose to overturn. But all these, and perhaps a hundred other microscopic species, seek shelter under boulders.

So—*PLEASE TURN BACK THOSE BOULDERS*, and do it *carefully*! It would be quite impossible to estimate the damage that could be caused by even one group of people on one low tide, wandering over a reef at midday and leaving over-turned boulders exposed to the hot tropical sun. This is one of the most important habitats on a reef, because it shelters representatives of practically every major group in the animal kingdom, either as eggs, larvae or adults. A fact which is either unknown or, sadly, is often completely ignored, especially by unscrupulous shell collectors.

There are many reefs on which every dead boulder may also be a haven for all sorts of boring animals, all competing for living space. The boulders appear dead, unexciting pieces of rock, but as the tide returns and the little burrowing Clams open their shell valves, expanding their mantles under water, to the sun, magically the drab surface becomes a blaze of rainbow-tinted colours.

Small Boring Clams open and spread their multi-coloured mantles as the rising tide covers the reef.

11 The Reef Crest

The Reef Crest, or the Algal Rim, which is a conspicuous feature on many reefs, is a smooth, pavement-like area just in from the reef's edge, and running parallel to it.

The waves pound unceasingly on this with great force, removing any boulders and leaving a bare region with few obvious signs of life. But this 'pavement' as it is called, has been constructed almost entirely by living plants, the red encrusting coralline algae. This group of seaweeds is of the greatest importance in the whole structure of any reef, adding tremendously to its stability.

The spores of these algae, of which there are several species, settle on dead coral and broken boulders, welding them into an almost unbreakable surface. Together with the calcareous (limy) remains of other reef animals and plants, there may be formed a solid encrustation, over a period of time, slightly higher than the surrounding area, and all along the crest of the reef.

Here the few obvious animals include the tough, spiky dark green Sea Cucumber, the brilliant Blue Starfish, or its smaller reddish brown relative.

Encrusting Coralline Algae are pinkish-mauve in colour and form a cement-like cover over broken coral fragments.

The Blue Starfish lives on the pavement-like reef crust along the outer edge of the reef.

SNORKEL IN A SAFE REEF EDGE POOL

Choose a shallow pool so you can stand on the bottom and look around with your mask and snorkel on. Map your pool with all its different coral types, multicoloured fishes, anemones, sea-stars.

12 The Edge of the Reef

The edge of the reef (southern shore).

Just seaward of the reef crest is the reef's edge — a place of magic — an exciting wonderland where you really feel that you are at last on a coral reef. For this is where you will find the living corals, massed in a fascinating array of colour, growing in profusion, either along the edge and down the reef's slope, or in deep blue pools. It is a place of rushing water as the ebbing tide cascades over the reef's edge.

Try to tread gently — take care where you walk — the fragile branching corals snap so easily. One group of people in a day can do almost as much damage as a cyclone, ruining perhaps a year's growth of coral. Be sure and keep a watchful eye for the turn of the tide, for the water races back across the reef flat and visibility may be poor.

The deeper coral pools along the edge are safe places for snorkelling. Just standing on the reef surface it is very easy to see the shoals of little fishes, of every shape and colour, darting for cover at the first sign of danger.

Around the margin of the pools or just over the reef's edge, the corals, slightly sheltered from the breaking waves above them, grow into massive colonies of large branching staghorns. Plate corals, flat foliose sheets of brilliant colour, massive colonies of brain or honeycomb corals, delicate yellow or pink branching forms, all growing side by side, competing for space and food.

There are caverns and caves for the more adventurous to explore. Lined with brilliantly coloured encrusting sponges and anemones, delicate hydroids, soft corals, fan corals and many other animals, these places are a wonder and a delight, a treasure house for the scuba diver and the underwater photographer, but a guide and experience are essential in venturing there.

A Coral pool near the edge of the reef gives a good idea of the variety of corals that grow in close association with one another.

29

13 The Living Corals

Once you have been to the edge of the reef, you will have seen the most important of all the animals of the reef community, the reef-building corals themselves.

With their amazing ability to extract salts from the sea water and to secrete a protective skeleton (of calcium carbonate), they could be described not only as the architects and designers, but also the construction engineers and builders of the reef.

These skeletons are sculptured in an infinite variety of forms, with such precise pattern and exquisite design in the different kinds of coral, that the scientist is able to use the skeletons as a very important means of classifying the corals into species. Skeletons range in size from small solitary 'cups', in which a single coral polyp lies, to solid, massive types, to slender branching, leaf-like and encrusting species, all of which are pure white in colour.

It must be remembered that the incredible range of colour to be seen in the corals is only in the living tissue. It is partly due to pigment cells in the outer layers of tissue, to filamentous red or green algae in the skeleton and also, most commonly, the yellow, brown, green and mauve shades of the corals are produced by the minute *Zooxanthellae* (the symbiotic plant cells) within the layers of tissue.

Egg-sperm bundles of coral being released. These drift in the sea until ready to settle as tiny polyps. (Photo: Peter Harrison)

Living coral. A colony of a bright mauve-coloured foliose coral in a pool on the reef flat.

Until the 1980s very little was known about the life history of corals. There is a larval stage, called a planula, which drifts in the sea until it is ready to settle. By this means corals are distributed from reef to reef. It was thought, from the few studies which have been made, that corals released the larvae at any time throughout the year.

In 1981, at James Cook University in Townsville, a group of young scientists who were studying different corals, made the very exciting discovery that all their corals were breeding at the one time. By 1983, they had found over one hundred different corals, all producing their little reproductive bundles of eggs and sperm, at the same time along different parts of the reef. In fact, they can now predict almost the hour of the day in which the corals will spawn. After fertilization the eggs soon develop into little planula larvae, which may drift for days or even weeks before a suitable place is found to settle as a tiny polyp.

However, corals also have another very successful means of reproducing themselves.

This fragile, delicately branched coral is found as small colonies growing a few centimetres below other corals on the reef flat.

Once the little polyp settles it immediately begins to secrete its skeleton, the tiny limy cup in which it lives. At the same time it buds off another polyp beside it and these continue to do the same thing. And so a coral colony is formed. All the pieces of coral we see today are made up of perhaps thousands of little cups, every shape and size, all joined together. Each little polyp has contributed its share of the skeleton.

There seems to be no explanation why we find perhaps as many as five to ten different kinds of coral all living successfully together on any square metre of reef. Obviously the first polyps were able to settle and survive. Apart from the *Zooxanthellae* (the microscopic algae living in the tissues of the coral), which aid in nourishing the colony, the coral polyps are what is known as

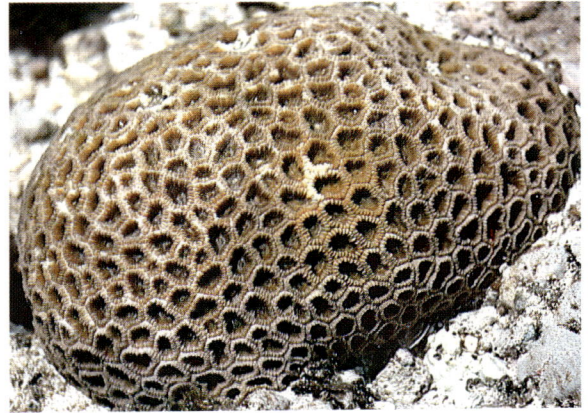

Honeycomb coral. This is one of the largest of the more solid, non-branching forms of coral.

plankton feeders. Their tiny tentacles, which have stinging cells in them, catch and paralyse minute animals which are being drifted over them in the water.

A Micro-atoll is formed when the coral colony reaches a sea level height at which it remains uncovered for long periods at low tide and the top surface dies allowing the centre to be eroded away.

Brain coral may form massive colonies. Its skeleton slightly resembles the surface of a brain, hence the common name.

The great branching staghorn corals in particular provide a safe retreat for hundreds of different kinds of little fishes.

It has been estimated that there are over three hundred different kinds of corals to be found in Barrier Reef waters. There are more than seventy different staghorn corals alone, and these are by far the most important of all the reef-building corals. Since they require well oxygenated water, they flourish best along the outer edges of the reef, and the best development of the larger, branching species, is just below the surface of the sea, beyond the greatest force of breaking waves.

Once the coral colonies have become established they provide both food and shelter for that great host of other animals and plants that go to make up the coral reef community.

Remember that all these corals are very brittle and break easily. *Don't tread on them*. Their edges are extremely sharp, *so don't handle them*. Coral cuts can be very painful and need careful treatment.

Skeleton of the Horse's Tooth Coral. Each massive cup has a long stalked base, the whole individual closely resembling the shape of a horse's tooth.

14 The Soft Corals

The word 'coral' has been used, and misused, in so many ways that it is perhaps necessary to explain the difference and the true meaning of the word in the scientific sense. The dead coral skeleton, too often painted in gaudy colours, collecting dust on someone's shelf, is 'coral' to many people.

The *true* corals are the skeleton-secreting kinds, all the reef-building species which zoologists group together in one section of the animal kingdom.

Distantly related to these reef-building corals, are a number of other reef animals which, with some kind of prefix added to them, are referred to as 'corals'. Some of these do play a small part in reef-building. While they may have a skeleton, this can be either hard or of horny material, quite different in composition to the true corals, and it is found within the tissues of the animal colony instead of just lying below the polyps. The other big difference, however, which easily distinguishes all these so-called 'corals' from the reef-builders, is that the polyps in each case all bear *eight* only pinnate (feathery) tentacles. All reef-building corals have either six, or multiples of six, tentacles.

The 'Soft' corals may be seen as large isolated colonies on the reef flat, or they may cover quite a large area where they have grown over dead coral. When the tide is out, the Soft corals look like a flat, leathery mass,

Where coral has died on a reef, the whole surface may be recolonized by soft corals.

Colonies of Soft corals may be found in all shapes, sizes and colours usually ranging through yellows, pale greens to fawn and grey. By day, at times of low tide, the tiny flower-like polyps are all withdrawn into the tough leathery matrix of the colony and emerge to feed with the rising tide. The polyps in the lower right hand corner are just beginning to expand, giving the colony a furry instead of a smooth leathery appearance.

usually a dull yellow or green in colour. But as the tide turns and the delicate little white polyps emerge to feed, they resemble a bed of exquisite tiny flowers.

The 'Stinging Coral' (it is called 'Fire' coral in the Caribbean Sea), grows among other corals along the reef's edge, and it does look like a true coral, brown in colour and yellow along the flat tops of its short upright plates. If examined with a hand lens, however, it will be seen that the surface is quite smooth with tiny white pores through which the microscopic polyps emerge to feed. The little polyps contain stinging cells which cause considerable irritation to the human skin.

The 'Red' coral (which was the 'Precious' coral of the Mediterranean Sea), and 'Black' coral, both of which are used extensively in jewellery making, are not found in intertidal reef waters and are rare on the Barrier Reef.

'Blue' coral is found only on reefs in the northern part of the Barrier Reef. In outward appearance it also resembles true coral.

Best known of these kinds of coral is perhaps the 'Organ-pipe' coral. Small colonies, often with their greenish-grey tentacles expanded during the day, can be seen on the reef flat at Heron Island.

Its polyps secrete a calcareous red, tube-like skeleton, each tube connected to the next, giving it the common name. Little bits of this skeleton are common among the shell debris along the shores of coral cays.

In all these 'false' corals, the colour is in the skeleton itself, and the colour remains permanently after the death of the colony.

Organ-pipe coral, which is related to the soft corals.

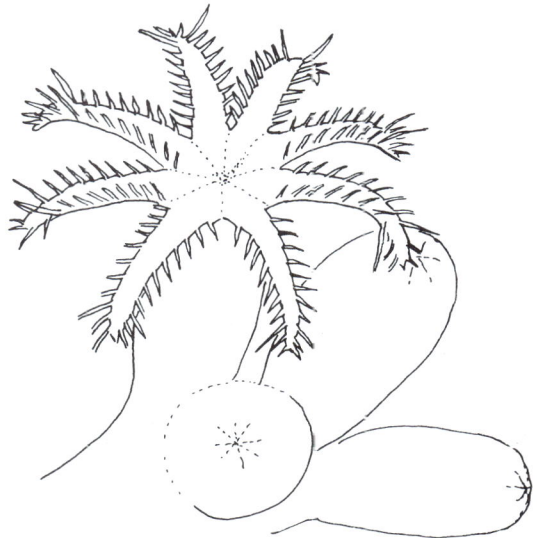

Diagram of soft coral polyp. Note only eight feathery tentacles.

15 Partnerships

In wading across a reef you will have been able to see that the animals and plants have taken advantage of every kind of place in which to live and grow. Seaweeds cover every dead boulder. The animals live in among the corals and in, on, or under dead boulders, buried in the sand or actively swimming, crawling over the sandy floor of pools, or scuttling among coral rubble.

There are also a number of fascinating associations which you may be able to see — certain kinds of animals living together or with a seaweed on the reef. It may be just a matter of seeking shelter, for one of the partners. Sometimes one partner helps the other, or gains a certain advantage for itself.

In almost every one of these partnerships the particular animal concerned is usually only found associated with a certain kind of animal or plant, and nowhere else on the reef.

Several of the small crabs are experts at finding a place to live, protected from predators. In some cases they have become so beautifully adapted in shape and colour, that they are almost invisible to the human eye. A pair of pale green crabs lives among the green Turtle Weed, while another pair, beautifully mottled grey and white, lives among the branches of the Soft coral *Xenia*. Another pair, with a body shaped to match its host, lives among the fronds of the green seaweed, *Halimeda*.

Fan worms, all the colours of the rainbow, settle as tiny larvae round the side of a coral colony.

Reef crab. Small crabs of every colour may be found under boulders or crawling among the corals on the reef flat.

Turtle weed. This vivid green seaweed is one of the most easily recognized algae on the reef flats.

Beautifully marked shrimps shelter among the tentacles of sand-burrowing anemones. Another is found among the mantle folds of the large colourful Magic Carpet, or Spanish Dancer Sea Slug. It is perhaps interesting to

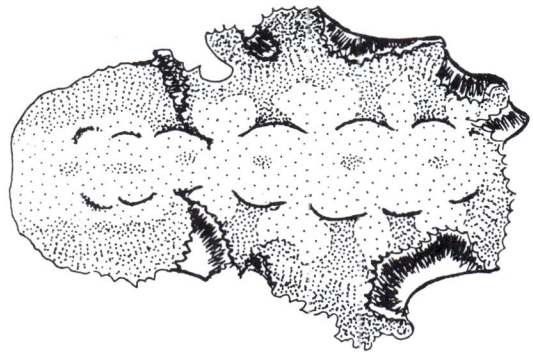

Spanish Dancer sea slug.

note that this particular shrimp has been found in this same Sea Slug in places as far distant as Zanzibar on the east coast of Africa, the Great Barrier Reef and the Hawaiian Islands.

Colourful Clown fishes may often be seen darting among the tentacles of large reef

A fascinating feature of the larger anemones is their association with certain small fish. Colourful little clown fish seek protection among the tentacles of the anemone.

anemones. They are not stung themselves but they lure other fishes to their doom.

If your visit to the reef happens to be at the time the turtles are coming ashore to lay, you may have the opportunity to examine one because the Marine Park officers are carrying out a research into the life history of these animals and sometimes bring them ashore during the day, to measure and tag them. Often the turtles have large white barnacles attached to their backs. These barnacles are creatures of the high seas, but they must have a solid base on which to settle and grow. The large smooth back of the turtle is an ideal home.

There are other 'free riders'. The large Remoras are fish which have a sucker-like disc on top of the head. They attach themselves to

Turtle barnacles. All barnacles must find a solid object on which to live, and the smooth hard back of a turtle can provide this.

sharks, Manta Rays and turtles, hitching a ride, and only dropping off to feed.

When snorkelling across the sandy areas of the reef at high tide, you may be fortunate enough to watch another interesting pair at work. A small Goby fish sits at the entrance to a burrow. If you wait quietly and patiently, you may see a Snapping shrimp emerge, pushing out the sand with its large claws. At the slightest sign of danger the watchful fish gives a signal and both disappear in a flash down the burrow.

Perhaps one of the most fascinating of all these associations is that of the 'cleaners'. You would probably only see this if snorkelling in a deep pool or over the edge of the reef. Beautiful blue and black striped fish, *Labroides*, and a delicate Banded Coral shrimp, each set up a 'cleaner station'.

Many fishes are irritated by parasites, which attach to their mouths or around the gills, and they have learnt how to rid themselves of the cause of their trouble. They come along to a station and stay patiently as the 'cleaners' remove the parasites. In providing an easy meal for the 'cleaners', the fishes benefit at the same time.

Banded Coral Shrimps. These colourful shrimps set up 'cleaning stations' where fish line up to be cleaned of parasites by the shrimps' tiny nippers. (Photo: Len Zell)

PARTNERSHIPS TO WATCH

Clown Fish Families
When snorkelling in the lagoon, in coral pools, near bommies or at the reef edge, you may find large anemones. Darting in among the tentacles will be small striped fish. Try to count how many in each anemone you see. Is there a pattern? Does the clown fish number depend on the size of the anemones?

Goby and shrimps
Snorkel over the reef flat and look for goby holes in the sand. When you find one, stand and watch it through your mask. Watch what the goby does. See if a shrimp appears cleaning out the hole.

Cleaner Stations
If you come across a cleaner station while snorkelling, note the cleaner fish. How many different fishes are lined up at the cleaner station?

16 The Fishes

Shoals of small fishes and many kinds of larger invertebrate animals seek shelter around coral colonies. (Photo: Ron & Valerie Taylor)

As you wander across the reef flat you will notice all sorts of small fish, diving for cover in holes in the sand, under boulders or among the branches of corals. The fishes, in every colour, shape and size, are as much a part of the reef community as the corals which bring them there, and they are amongst its most fascinating inhabitants.

Fishes are found in all the varied habitats on the reef. The larger sharks, and other carnivorous fish, haunt the reef's margins. Many fish, with brilliant colours and often bizarre shapes, Box Fish, Butterfly Cod, Anemone Fish, Moorish Idols, Chaetodons and Demoselles, live in their selected areas on

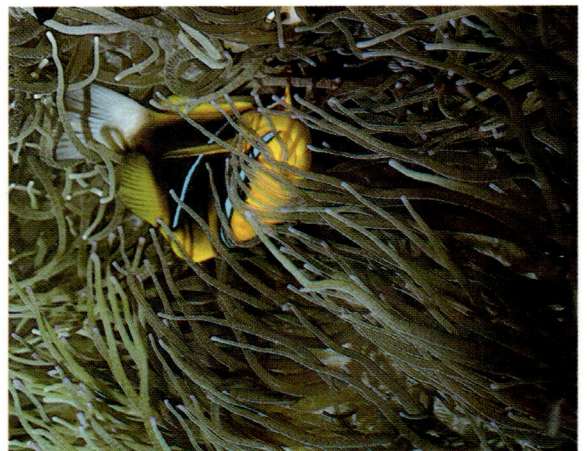

Little anemone fish live among the tentacles of large anemones. (Photo: Ron & Valerie Taylor)

the reef—in pools, in anemones, and among the branching corals, seeking either protection or food. Browsing species return over the reef with the rising tide.

Shoals of large bright blue and green Parrot fish, vivid in the tropical sunlight, invade the reef flats. Their effect, on both the larger and the microscopic algae on the reef, may cause all sorts of unexpected changes. These Parrot fish, with their strong, beak-like teeth, rasp algae from the beach rock and coral boulders, but they may also prey on living coral colonies, consuming both the coral tissue and the skeleton. The latter is returned to the reef floor as sediments, but in their feeding activities the Parrot fish may also destroy thousands of newly settled corals and other animals.

Large fish prey on smaller fish, which in turn prey on smaller animals, including fish larvae. Normally there is a harmonious balance among the different kinds, but people prey on them all. There are commercial fisheries for large, fast-swimming fish like

A quaint little Boxfish (Photo: Ron & Valerie Taylor)

Many kinds of beautifully marked Butterfly fish live among the corals (Photo: Ron & Valerie Taylor)

This beautifully marked little Epaulette shark, very often seen on the reef flats, was first described by members of Captain Cook's crew from the Endeavour River.

The large gentle Manta Ray swims gracefully through the water trapping tiny plankton animals in its large mouth (Photo: L. Zell)

Tuna and Mackerel, in open waters between the reefs. Many choice, edible species, such as Coral Trout and Red Emperor, are caught by handline round the reef margins. There is a Big Game Fishery for Sharks and Marlin off Cairns at certain times of the year although, fortunately, most Marlin caught are tagged and released.

Since the Great Barrier Reef Marine Park Authority was set up and many areas proclaimed as Marine National Parks, certain restrictions have been placed on selected reefs in regard to fishing. In order to find out about life histories—where fish breed and how many there are, especially of the better edible species—studies are still being carried out in a number of areas in the Great Barrier Reef. Where it is found that a certain reef is being too heavily fished, or is perhaps a good breeding ground, that particular reef may be either closed to fishing for a period of time, or completely closed. By this means it is hoped to conserve the various fish populations.

There is also a constant demand for exotic fish for home aquaria. By issuing licences to approved collectors only, it is hoped to prevent too many of these fish being removed from the reefs.

The Red Emperor is considered to be one of the finest edible fishes of the reefs. (Photo: Ron & Valerie Taylor)

FISH FANATICS

First make an underwater slate:

Look around for something waterproof, light coloured and with a rough surface which you can write on with pencil. An offcut of laminex or formica works well. Even a white tile can be used. If you can, attach a pencil.

Another way is to bring waterproof drafting film and clamp it onto a plastic board.

Now with snorkel, mask, fins, underwater slate and pencil you can join the fish fanatics. The hardest thing is to concentrate on just one of these fish at a time. Carefully note down its markings, colours and behaviour. When you get back to shore, use colours to finish the fish markings and then see if you can find it using reference books from a library.

The Great Barrier Reef, with its hundreds of reefs and cays, is one of the richest areas in the world for sea birds, and twenty-two different species breed there. Their importance in the general ecology of coral islands cannot be stressed enough. They are the means, through their droppings, by which organic food material in the sea is transferred to the land, the link in the building up and stabilization of the coral cays, fertilizing the sands, thus enabling the establishment of the grasses, creepers and the trees. They are also, in many cases, the means by which plant seeds are carried from island to island.

Whilst the sea birds depend on the coral cays as *land* mass for resting and nesting, in contrast to the surrounding reefs and waters

Bramble Cay. As the only speck of land in a large area of sea, this tiny cay is the resting and nesting place of thousands of sea birds.

Brown Gannets, or Boobies, take off from the shores of an isolated cay in the Swain Reefs.

with their large populations of marine animals, it should be remembered that these birds are also entirely dependent on the sea for their food.

Birds such as Gannets, Terns and Cormorants, dive for fish. Others like the Shearwaters (the Mutton Birds), skim the surface of the sea for tiny planktonic animals. Reef Herons and Oyster Catchers stalk across the reef flat at low water seeking their prey, and the Sea Gulls scavenge along the shore.

While some birds remain near the shore to feed, like the Terns, others such as the Mutton Birds and Gannets may range far out to sea. Many of the Terns, the Lesser Frigate Bird and the Gannets nest on bare ground. Others, like the White-capped Noddy, build untidy nests in trees.

However, it is the Wedge-tailed Shearwater, the Mutton Bird, which has the greatest impact on a coral cay during the breeding season. These birds, so clumsy on land and amongst the most graceful of fliers at sea, only come ashore for the spring and summer months. Their nests are at the end of burrows, up to over a metre in length. In a

Brown Gannet and chick. The fluffy white down of the chick makes it appear larger than its parent.

Masked Gannet colony on Gannet Cay, Swain Reefs. This gannet tends to stay on the far outer reefs.

45

The 'Mutton Bird' or Wedge-tailed Shearwater, at the entrance to its burrow among the roots of a *Pisonia* tree.

Black or White-capped Noddy on its nest, Heron Island.

Sooty Terns on Michaelmas Cay. In the breeding season various species of terns occupy all the available land space. (Photo: Lloyd Grigg)

Frigate Bird colony, Bell Cay, Swain Reefs. Sometimes called 'the Pirates of the Pacific', these birds have the greatest wing span in relation to the weight of their bodies of all birds

large breeding colony, the tunnels the birds make may cover the whole area under the trees, making walking across a cay an hazardous adventure, and sometimes resulting in the crushing of an egg or chick. As dusk falls, the Mutton Birds begin to arrive. Their weird and wonderful mating cries continue throughout the night, making sleep impossible for some visitors. At the very first light of dawn, one of each pair departs for the feeding grounds. This is a sight which should not be missed. The birds have special 'runways' and all line up to take off at speed.

The size of any breeding colony depends to a large extent on the availability of food. On Michaelmas Cay, out from Cairns, the Sooty Terns breed in their tens of thousands on the bare ground. On Heron Island, the Black (or White-capped) Noddy, nests in the low shrubs or high up in the trees, again in the thousands, completely undaunted by the presence of tourists. It lays its egg on its flat, untidy nest of dead leaves, sitting precariously on the swaying branches.

The Masked Gannet and the Frigate Bird seek the distant cays among the outer reefs, far from human habitation.

In the summer months, migrants from distant lands in the northern hemisphere, the waders such as Turnstones, Tattlers, Godwits and some of the Plovers, forage along the shoreline.

With the new National Park regulations, some of the cays which are known to be important breeding grounds for certain species of birds, are listed as completely closed all year or at least during the breeding season — spring and summer.

18 The Sea Turtles

The Sea Turtles are the largest animals to be seen on a coral cay and their story is a fascinating one. While many of the sea birds may be seen on the shingle banks and cays all through the year, the turtles only come ashore in the spring and early summer to lay their eggs.

There are six different species of sea turtles in the waters of the Great Barrier Reef, but only three are at all common. Only two of these, the Green and Loggerhead turtles, breed as far south as Heron and other islands of the Capricorn Group. This area is one of two major nesting grounds. The other is Raine Island in the far north.

The male turtle never leaves the sea. The female comes ashore at night and struggles laboriously through the soft sand to make her nest above the beach. She remains only a few hours, just long enough to lay her eggs, anything from fifty to 200 at a time, before returning to the sea. Having chosen her nesting site, the turtle proceeds, with great effort, to thrash around until she has formed a large pit. In the centre of this she then digs a round, deep hole, with her hind flippers, in which to lay her ping-pong ball sized eggs. She may come ashore to lay several times in one season.

Depending upon whether the nest has been made in the open or in deep shade under a tree, the eggs will take from eight to ten weeks to hatch. As the tiny hatchlings emerge from the nest, usually at night, they

Green Turtle hatchlings racing down the beach to the water in the early dawn.

make for the region of most light, the open sky, and thus to the sea. At night their greatest enemy is the Ghost Crab. Should they emerge during the day, they fall an easy prey to the Gulls, Reef Herons and large fish.

One of the greatest fascinations of a visit to a coral cay in the months from October to March, is to find the tell-tale tracks of the turtle, follow them up the beach and watch her proceed to make her nest and lay her eggs.

Fortunately today, where tourist resorts are located on turtle-nesting cays, every precaution is being taken to create as little disturbance as possible to the turtles. On Heron Island, for example, where the Queensland Marine Park biologists are making a long-term study of reef turtles. Turtles are caught during the day and brought in to the beach to be measured, weighed and tagged, before being returned to the sea. As they

Turtles' tracks on Bramble Cay

Turtle weighing on Heron Island.

49

A large female Green Turtle returns to the sea at dawn after laying her eggs high up in the sand.

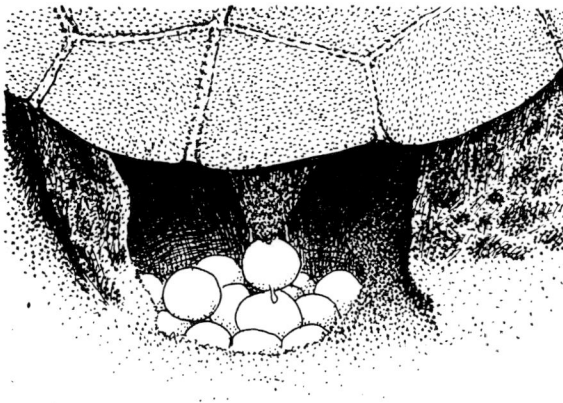

Turtle dropping eggs into hole.

work the biologists give to interested visitors a description of what they are doing and the reasons for doing it.

At night they give lectures or lead groups of people along the beach to watch and perhaps photograph. People are warned never to approach closely until the turtle has actually begun to lay, to keep silent and not to use torches. The lights of the resort can distract and confuse a turtle should she come ashore in the vicinity of the buildings. Getting her flippers caught in the beach rock is another hazard the turtle has to face.

Marine turtles round the world have been slaughtered for food, and for by-products such as leather and tortoise-shell. Their nests have been robbed of the eggs for food. In South-east Asia alone human predation of turtle eggs and hatchlings has been estimated as high as 40% of the total laying.

Today all species of turtles are protected in Queensland—only the Aboriginal and Island peoples being permitted to continue their traditional hunting. There were turtle soup factories in the Capricorn Islands in the 1920s—in 1924 over 1200 animals were killed on North West Island alone.

A small six-month old Loggerhead Turtle reared at Heron Island. With its larger head and sculptured back, it is easily distinguished from the tiny black and white Green Turtles.

The Great Barrier Reef Green Turtle population may be the last of the world's great Green Turtle herds. Raine Island, far out on the northern outer Barrier, is recognized as a major world nesting place for turtles (and for sea birds), and in the year 1974 biologists recorded about 11,500 turtles coming ashore to nest during one night.

Although much has now been learnt about turtles, hidden in the sea as they are, they are difficult animals to study. There are still many questions not fully answered—just how long do they live, where and how far do they travel, and how many times do they breed? Each year, the long-term study being carried out by the Queensland National Parks and Wildlife Services biologists, bring new facts to light and the story is gradually being put together.

TRACKING TURTLES

If you are visiting the reef islands between October and March, become a turtle tracker. Find out the difference between tracks going up the beach from the water and tracks leading back to the water.

Keep an eye out for tiny tracks of hatchlings. If you find some, see if you can work out how many hatchlings scurried down that way.

19 The Mammals

Visitors to the Great Barrier Reef are more familiar with fishes, sea birds and turtles as vertebrate animals forming a large part of the enormous animal communities of the reefs. But there are three other much larger, warm-blooded vertebrates to be found in Barrier Reef waters. Unfortunately most are rarely seen.

The graceful and playful Dolphins are found along all parts of the east Australian coast, and are now well-known to most people. Great excitement is caused when two or three of these powerful swimmers catch the bow wave of a launch and sometimes continue for quite long distances to enjoy a free ride.

However, it is not generally realized that one of their larger relatives, the gentle Humpback Whale, migrates each year from the far Southern Ocean. About May, the whales make their long 5,000 kilometre swim north along the coast to the warm sheltered waters of the Barrier Reef to mate and, in the following year, to give birth to their young. This ensures that the new-born calves, which do not have a protective layer of blubber at that age, don't have to face the icy Antarctic seas in the first months of their lives. The southward return journey begins about July or August, continuing until about October.

There was a fishery for these migrating whales at Twofold Bay, on the far south coast of New South Wales, about the middle of the last century and this was carried on in a small way into the early 1910s. Much later, more modern methods of catching these whales was carried out from Byron Bay, in northern New South Wales, and later from Tangalooma on Moreton Island in south Queensland. Intensive catching resulted in the

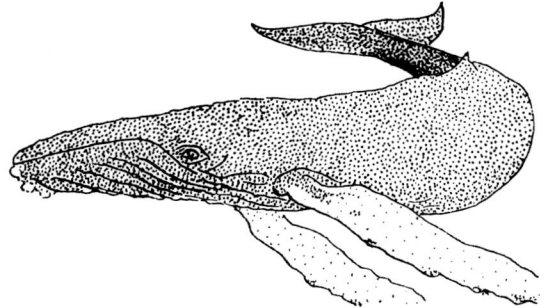
Humpback whale

Dolphin

whale numbers being so reduced that the fishery was forced to close down.

Happily the numbers are increasing each year now, and with world-wide demands for the protection of all whales, the future of the Humpback Whales in Barrier Reef waters seems assured.

The Dugong (or Sea Cow), is another large, gentle mammal, which makes its home in Barrier Reef waters. Where sea grasses flourish, herds of these curious mammals are to be found. In many parts of the world they have been hunted almost to extinction, but today these unique animals are rigorously protected in Australian seas. The Islanders and the Aborigines, their traditional hunters, are now required to have permits to capture them for food. Officers of the Great Barrier Reef Marine Park Authority are working with these people, explaining the reasons for limiting the catch, and gaining their cooperation in conserving stocks for the future.

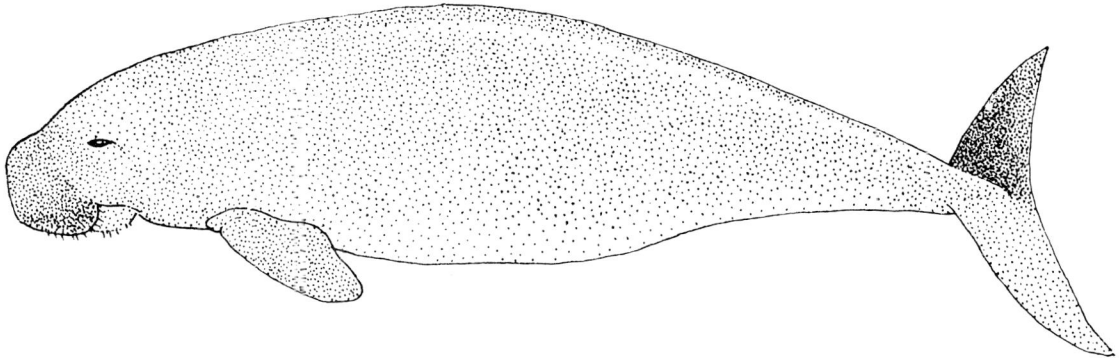

Dugong

WHALES, DOLPHINS AND DUGONGS

If you're lucky enough to see any Marine Mammals—Whales, Dolphins or Dugong, record the date, time, place of sighting, number, estimate of size, direction of travel and if there are any young.

The Dolphins most likely to be seen are: Bottle-nosed Dolphins, Common Dolphins, Pilot Whales and False Killer Whales. Watching dolphins riding the bow waves of boats is great fun.

20 People and the Great Barrier Reef

Historical

Before the known arrival of the first white man, the Australian Aborigines, who lived along the shores of the coast of Queensland, collected oysters and other molluscs and caught fish, turtles and Dugong.

They were not, however, a sea-going people like the fierce warriors of the Torres Strait Islands with their great war canoes. Most of the bark canoes of the coastal tribes were only large enough for one or two people. Also they were fragile craft which would be unseaworthy in all but very calm weather.

There is evidence that there were settlements on a number of islands within reef waters, and it is certainly known that they ventured as far afield as the Lizard Island Group on fishing trips, probably visiting many other islands lying close to the mainland coast.

But with their small numbers, and the great distance between many of the reefs, there is no doubt that those first Australians posed no threats to the Great Barrier Reef.

On the 11 June 1770, the small ship, H.M.Bark *Endeavour*, under Lieut. James Cook R.N., went aground on the reef which today bears her name.

The first detailed description of the coastline of the State of Queensland, and of many of the islands offshore, is to be found in Cook's *Journal* of that voyage. A glance at the map, which accompanies his *Journal*, will show the number of capes, bays and islands, all well-known today, which still bear the names given by Cook during that voyage.

Among those on board were the famous botanist, Sir Joseph Banks, and his assistants, the Swedish naturalist, Solander, and the Scottish artist, Parkinson. To them we owe our first descriptions and illustrations of many of the plants and animals of eastern Australia.

The Steamer Track

Since sailing through the great maze of reefs and islands of Great Barrier Reef waters requires both knowledge and careful navigation, it will be appreciated that it has been very necessary to have correct information regarding depths, submerged reefs and tidal range.

Today, there is marked on all charts, the 'Steamer Track'. For the greater part of its length, this charted track lies along the Queensland coast in a narrow zone comparatively free from coral. Throughout a voyage from Brisbane to Torres Strait, there

H.M. Barque *Endeavour*

Naturalist group on Shingle Beach, Wilson Island.

Small fast runabouts such as this one now crowd Barrier Reef waters. (Photo: J. Field)

is very little indication that a ship will have passed through reef-strewn waters. Only by studying the charts during the voyage, and following along the shipping lanes of this 'Inner Route', can a passenger begin to understand the magnitude of the reefs and islands which surround it.

In the far northern region, where the continental shelf is very narrow, with the outermost reefs lying only about twenty-five kilometres from the mainland, the reefs, which are numerous and not far apart, are visible from the deck of a passing ship. With the sun at the right angle, large patches of pale green colour against a deep blue, indicate the presence of submerged reefs.

Tourism

Until the 1930s there were no tourist resorts, as we know them today, on any of the Barrier Reef Islands, and it was to be

Tourist launches available for charter in Barrier Reef waters.

People turning over boulder.

many years before the real possibilities for tourist traffic were fully appreciated.

By 1970 there were resorts on nine of the coral cays and mainland islands. Today the number has risen to seventeen and others are being planned.

The advent of high-powered, small craft, along the Queensland coast, brought many previously untouched reefs and islands into contact with ever increasing numbers of fishermen and campers.

Glass-bottomed boats, underwater observatories, scuba diving gear, and most recently, submersible craft, have all opened up, to a far wider viewing, all the magnificent life of the coral reefs.

Few of the people using small craft realize the enormous damage anchors can do to reef corals. The number of boats among the reefs is increasing rapidly each year. Yacht races are being held and wind-surfing competitions promoted to lure people to the resorts. More and more charter boats are being added, sailing out from a number of mainland towns, and landing people on reefs which were previously inaccessible. It is both difficult and dangerous to land on the edge of a reef from a small launch or dinghy, and much of the fragile branching corals will be broken in the process.

The accommodation standards required by overseas visitors have resulted in the development of much more sophisticated resorts, and the addition of more and more buildings. Fast transport, by helicopters and aeroplanes, has to a large extent replaced the more leisurely launch trips, necessitating the building of landing strips, and thus taking up even more land on the small islands.

Attempts are being made to restrict uncontrolled development, to limit it to places that are not vital to the preservation of the

Heron Island, Western end, showing guesthouse complex and research station.

Pollution from people will be a growing problem. (Photo: J. Field)

reef communities. But, at the same time, trying to make it possible for all people to have the opportunity of seeing a little of our coral wonderland.

Pollution

Controversial subjects such as drilling for oil, mining for coral sand, the dumping of silt into clear waters, the outbreak of the large populations of the coral-eating Crown of Thorns Starfish, and the resulting damage to reefs, have all been given wide coverage by both newspapers and television. The result has been that the whole region of the Great Barrier Reef was brought to the notice of the general public as never before.

Large oil tankers, with greatly increased draught, were using the Steamer Track inside the reefs, since this is a shorter route and

58

therefore less costly than sailing outside to the east. And so there is the ever-present possibility of a large oil spill with its tragic aftermath, especially in the narrow northern region with its four to five metre rise and fall of tide and its closely scattered reefs. In terms of destructive power, shipping is perhaps more a threat to the reefs than the reefs are to shipping.

The tanker *Oceanic Grandeur* of 58,000 dwt with a draught of between ten and twelve metres, struck an uncharted pinnacle in the middle of the main shipping lane in Torres Strait on the 3 March 1970. Eight of its fifteen holds were punctured, and only the most extra-ordinary good fortune of calm weather and the presence of another tanker in ballast, saved a repetition of the *Torrey Canyon* disaster in the English channel in 1967, when the tanker went aground on the rocks. It would be impossible to calculate the damage which could be caused if such a disaster occurred in rough weather in northern reef waters, far from any adequate facilities to cope with such an event.

HOW YOU CAN HELP

Planning is necessary to ensure that tourist facilities on the Great Barrier Reef cater for the needs of tourists but do not affect the natural environment people come to see.

During your visit make a note of the best things about your visit. Also note anything you feel is spoiling, or could in the future spoil, the natural beauty of the area. If you are staying in a resort, write a letter to the management and tell them these things. This could help them plan for the future. If you are camping or sailing, write to the Great Barrier Reef Marine Park Authority and tell them. Management bodies like these need to get feedback from visitors.

The reef is very large, very diverse and there is still so much unknown. You can help.

The Great Barrier Reef Marine Park Authority needs records of all Crown of Thorns Starfish seen anywhere on the reefs. You would need to give the location and date, and record the numbers, size and whether there was evidence of feeding on nearby corals.

You can record sightings of whales—their numbers, size and description of any activity such as blowing or diving.

You can make your own records of the different kinds of birds you see on a coral island. Are they nesting, resting or feeding? Some feed at sea, others along the shoreline or on the reef as the tide goes down. Take your tape recorder too.

If you are on an island when turtles are nesting, record the kind and number of turtles nesting each night, the date and the location on the cay.

21 Research

The growth of scientific knowledge of the Great Barrier Reef has been slow and gradual. Quite large collections of some groups of animals from isolated reefs have been made, either by expeditions or small groups of people, and there are large collections, especially of shells and coral skeletons, scattered in museums throughout the world.

In the early days of Australia there were very few scientists, or ships, and distances were vast. It was not until the year 1893, that all the known facts were gathered together for the first time in a large book with beautiful black and white illustrations. It was called *The Great Barrier Reef of Australia, Its Products and Potentialities*, and was written by W. Saville Kent, then Commissioner of Fisheries in the Queensland Government, who explored many parts of the region.

There were a few concerned people, mostly scientists, who knew and appreciated the significance of this magnificent collection of reefs and islands, but were also very aware how little was known about them. In 1922, a Great Barrier Reef Committee was formed in Brisbane, with people from Australia and Great Britain meeting together to try and decide what was best for the future of the reef. There were geologists, geographers, botanists and zoologists and they all knew that nothing could be properly planned until a great deal more was known of the nature of the reefs, and the animal and plant communities which inhabited them.

As a result of their efforts a Great Barrier Reef Expedition went to Low Isles, about fourteen kilometres north-east of the Queensland town of Port Douglas, in 1929. The members mainly came from Britain and they were joined, for varying periods, by

Towing gear behind the Lizard Island research vessel (Photo: J. Field)

scientists from Australian universities and museums. A whole year was spent studying the reef in all its aspects, and when possible, visits were made to other reefs for comparison. The results of these studies were published in a series of reports by the British Museum (Natural History) London.

After this first basic study, a handful of scientists continued to work on the Reef, but there was no co-ordination of effort, each person working on the particular aspect which interested them, whether it was the geology, the plants, or some of the animals. Dedicated members of the Great Barrier Reef Committee continued in their efforts to awaken public interest, and to obtain Government action.

By the beginning of the 1970s, the situation began to change radically. In April, 1970, the Commonwealth Government brought into operation the Continental Shelf (Living Natural Resources) Act of 1968, which gave it control of this area in accordance with International Law. This Act

Students and scientists at work in the laboratory at Lizard Island (Photo: J. Field)

covered all the major invertebrate animal groups including Sponges, Corals and their relatives, Crustaceans, Molluscs and Echinoderms.

At the same time one of the largest research projects came into being with the establishment of the Australian Institute of Marine Research at Cape Cleveland, Townsville. Today a large group of scientists, and many overseas visitors, are working on all sorts of problems associated with the biology, geology and ecology of the reef communities.

22 The Great Barrier Reef Marine Park Authority

In response to people's growing awareness of the Reef's value as a unique national asset, and the widespread concern for its continued uncontrolled use, the Commonwealth Government's Great Barrier Reef Marine Park Act became Law on 20 June, 1975. Since an overall plan for the administration and development of the Great Barrier Reef as a whole had become absolutely essential, this Act was designed to ensure the control, care and development of the Reef as a national treasure, to be used and enjoyed by today's generation. But also to be maintained, with a minimum of disturbance to its natural state, so that it may still be used and enjoyed by all future generations.

In 1976, under the above Act, the Great Barrier Reef Marine Park Authority was brought into being. This Authority has the duty of recommending specified areas within the Great Barrier Reef to be set aside as Marine Parks.

It has the aid of a Consultative Committee, which has wide representation of all scientific, conservation and Government bodies concerned in any way with the future of the Reef, and whose members are chosen after close consultation between the Commonwealth and Queensland Governments.

The Authority's first duty was to prepare Zoning Plans which will cover both the continued use and protection of the Reefs. In preparing a plan, consideration has to be taken of all the reefs and islands within the selected area, and the way in which they are being used at this time. It involves a wide knowledge of both plants and animals, special consideration being given to the breeding grounds of the latter. Public meetings have been called and all members of the public with any special interest in the area are asked to participate, to state their requirements, or their ideas — whether they be commercial fishermen, tourist resort operators, sporting bodies or others. Then, before that Area can be officially proclaimed as a Marine Park, with each island or reef within it set aside for its special use, the Zoning Plan has to be put before another public meeting for its final acceptance.

In October 1981, the Great Barrier Reef was included in the World Heritage List and to date Proclamations have been made covering all the important sections. Many of the islands have been declared National Parks for years, and the control and management of both the National Parks and the Marine Parks will be in the hands of the Queensland National Parks and Wildlife Service and the Marine Park Authority. The protection and conservation of animals, especially in the sea, are a vexed and extremely difficult problem, and policing them over such an enormous area as the Great Barrier Reef, is virtually a physical impossibility.

Officers of the National Parks Service, who are based in Cairns and Rockhampton, patrol these sections using boats and planes to check the reefs and islands in the different sections. The number and kinds of boats within an area, the camps on islands, and other details, are recorded on each surveillance flight.

On Heron Island, an Information Centre is being set up with permanent Rangers whose duty, apart from research projects and surveillance, will be to give talks and advice to tourists.

Great Barrier Reef Marine Park
Capricornia Section

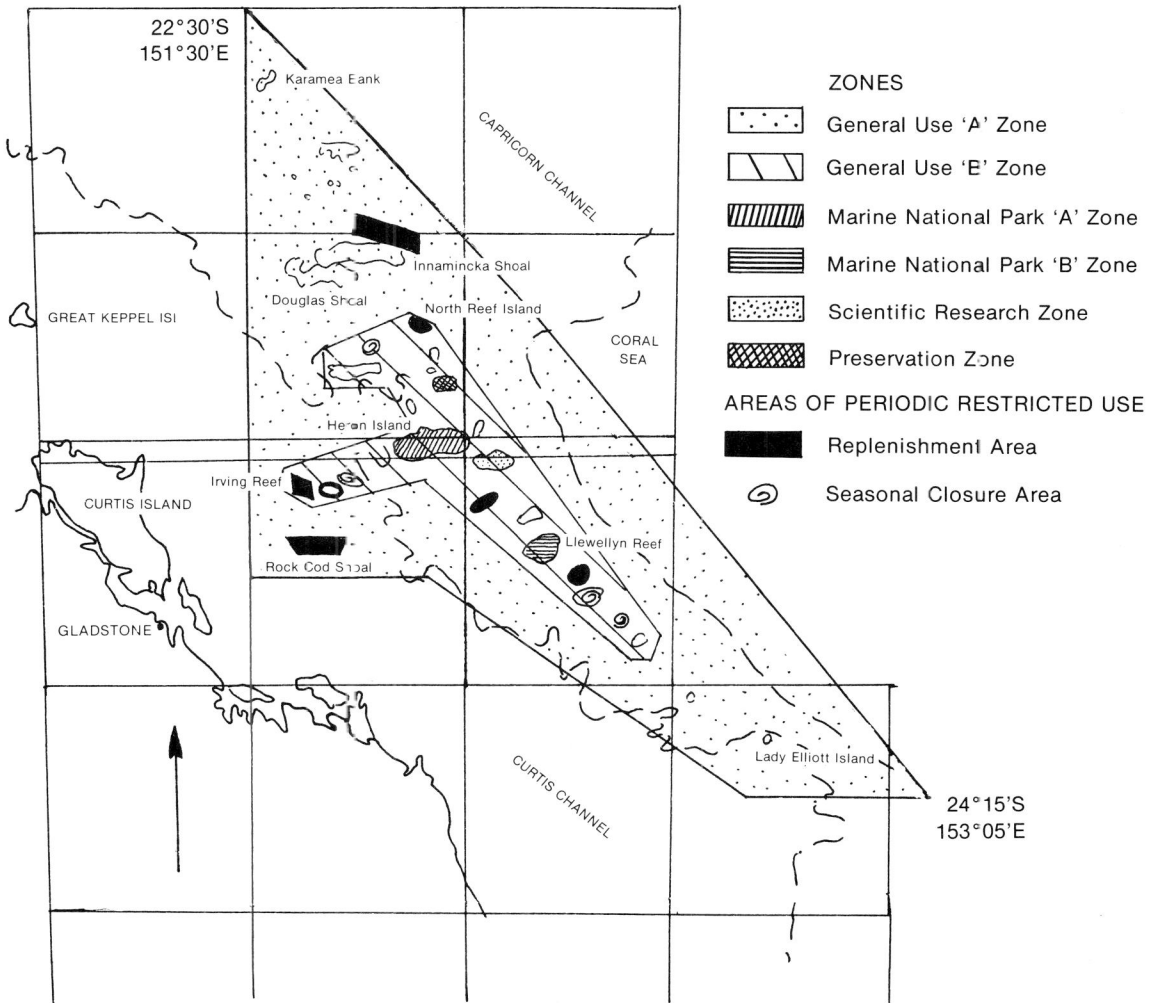

ZONES

∷∷∷	General Use 'A' Zone
╱╱╱	General Use 'B' Zone
▨▨▨	Marine National Park 'A' Zone
▤▤▤	Marine National Park 'B' Zone
░░░	Scientific Research Zone
▩▩▩	Preservation Zone

AREAS OF PERIODIC RESTRICTED USE

■	Replenishment Area
◎	Seasonal Closure Area

Map labels: 22°30'S 151°30'E, Karamea Bank, CAPRICORN CHANNEL, Innamincka Shoal, Douglas Shoal, North Reef Island, GREAT KEPPEL ISl, CORAL SEA, Heron Island, Irving Reef, CURTIS ISLAND, Llewellyn Reef, Rock Cod Shoal, GLADSTONE, Lady Elliott Island, CURTIS CHANNEL, 24°15'S 153°05'E

It is imperative that all Australians should learn to understand and appreciate the immensity of one of their greatest national assets. The Great Barrier Reef is one of the world's truly magnificent reservoirs of tropical islands and coral reefs, and it will only be with the help and co-operation of all Australians that the aims of the Authority can be achieved and the future of the Reef assured.

Books for Further Reading

BENNETT, ISOBEL (1984)   *The Great Barrier Reef.* (Lansdowne, Sydney)

FRANKEL, E. (1978)   *Bibliography of the Great Barrier Reef.* (Great Barrier Reef Marine Park Authority, Townsville).

HOPLEY, D. (1982)   *Geomorphology of the Great Barrier Reef.* (John Wiley & Sons, New York.)

KENCHINGTON, R.A. & HUDSON, BRYDGET E.T. (1984) (Editors) *Coral Reef Management Handbook.* (UNESCO, Jakarta)

MARSH, HELENE (1984) (Editor) *The Dugong* James Cook University of North Queensland, Townsville).

MATHER, PATRICIA & BENNETT, ISOBEL (1984) (Editors) *A Coral Reef Handbook.* (The Australian Coral Reef Society, Brisbane).

VERON, J.E.N. (1986)   *Corals of Australia and the Indo-Pacific.* (Angus & Robertson, Sydney)